Animal Atlas

Anna Claybourne
Illustrated by Christina Wald

A & C BLACK
AN IMPRINT OF BLOOMSBURY
LONDON   NEW DELHI   NEW YORK   SYDNEY

First published 2014 by
A & C Black, an imprint of Bloomsbury Publishing Plc
50 Bedford Square, London, WC1B 3DP

www.bloomsbury.com

Copyright © 2014 A & C Black
Text copyright © 2014 Anna Claybourne
Illustrations copyright © 2014 Christina Wald

ISBN 978-1-4088-4218-8

A CIP catalogue for this book is available from the British Library.

This book is produced using paper that is made from wood grown
in managed, sustainable forests. It is natural, renewable and
recyclable. The logging and manufacturing processes conform to the
environmental regulations of the country of origin.

Printed and bound in China by C & C Offset Printing Co., Ltd

1 3 5 7 9 10 8 6 4 2

Contents

World of animals

We live in a world full of amazing wild animals. Across the Earth's continents and oceans are vast areas of wilderness that are home to all sorts of creatures – wolves, elephants, albatrosses and armadillos, sharks, stingrays and thousands more. Even in a park or garden there are wild birds, butterflies, spiders, squirrels and other creatures – some of which even share our own homes.

How many?

Altogether, scientists have discovered and named just over a million different species, or types, of animals (as well as many more plants and other living things such as bacteria). However, this is just the start, as we are constantly discovering new species, especially in places like remote jungles and in the deep oceans. Scientists estimate that there are probably at least eight million different animals out there – we just don't know about most of them yet!

Habitat homes

The world is made up of many different types of landscapes and surroundings. This books shows just some of the animals found in continents across the world. Each animal is suited to the particular type of surrounding, or habitat, it lives in. The maps in this book show the following habitats:

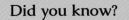

Habitats

Desert: Dry areas with not much rainfall

Forests: From hot and steamy rainforests to conifer and pine forests in cold places

Grassland: Savannas, prairies, steppes and pampas are all types of grasslands

Frozen land and snow: Frozen land and oceans

Mountains: Places that are very high above sea level

Seashore and oceans: Oceans, seas, and costal areas

Did you know?
Most of the one million or so animal species are insects and other creepy crawlies – in fact, a quarter of all types of animals are beetles!

5

World map

This map of the world shows where the main types of habitat are found, as well as all the Earth's continents and oceans.

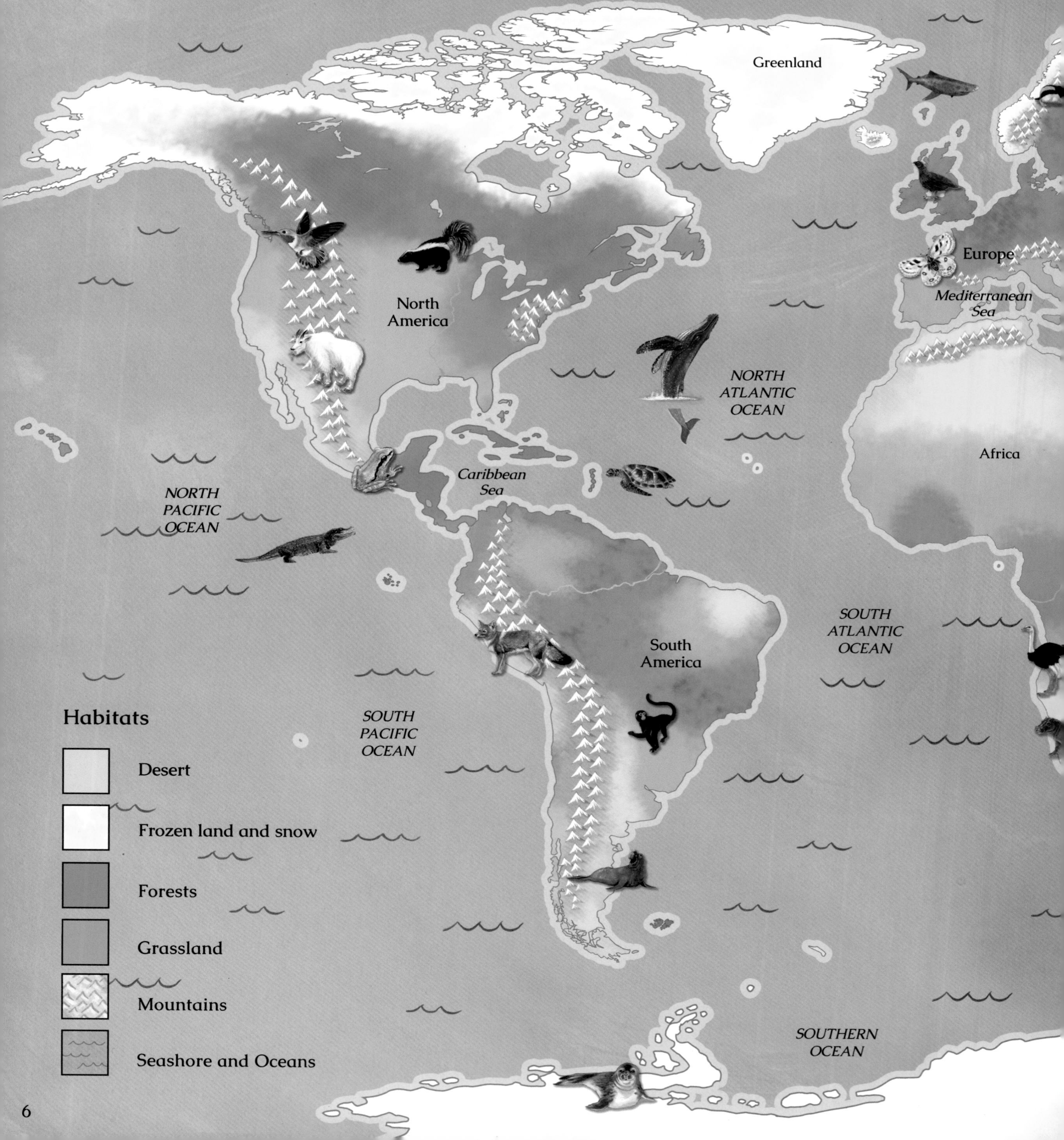

Arctic Ocean

Greenland

North America

Europe

Mediterranean Sea

NORTH ATLANTIC OCEAN

Africa

NORTH PACIFIC OCEAN

Caribbean Sea

SOUTH ATLANTIC OCEAN

South America

SOUTH PACIFIC OCEAN

Habitats

- Desert
- Frozen land and snow
- Forests
- Grassland
- Mountains
- Seashore and Oceans

SOUTHERN OCEAN

Highest mountain: Mount Everest, Asia: 8,850 m (29,035 feet)
Biggest lake: Lake Superior, North America: 82,100 km2 (31,700 square miles)
Longest river: River Nile, Africa: around 6,800 km (4,250 miles)

Asia

Black
Sea

Caspian
Sea

NORTH
PACIFIC
OCEAN

INDIAN
OCEAN

Oceania

SOUTH
PACIFIC
OCEAN

Antarctica

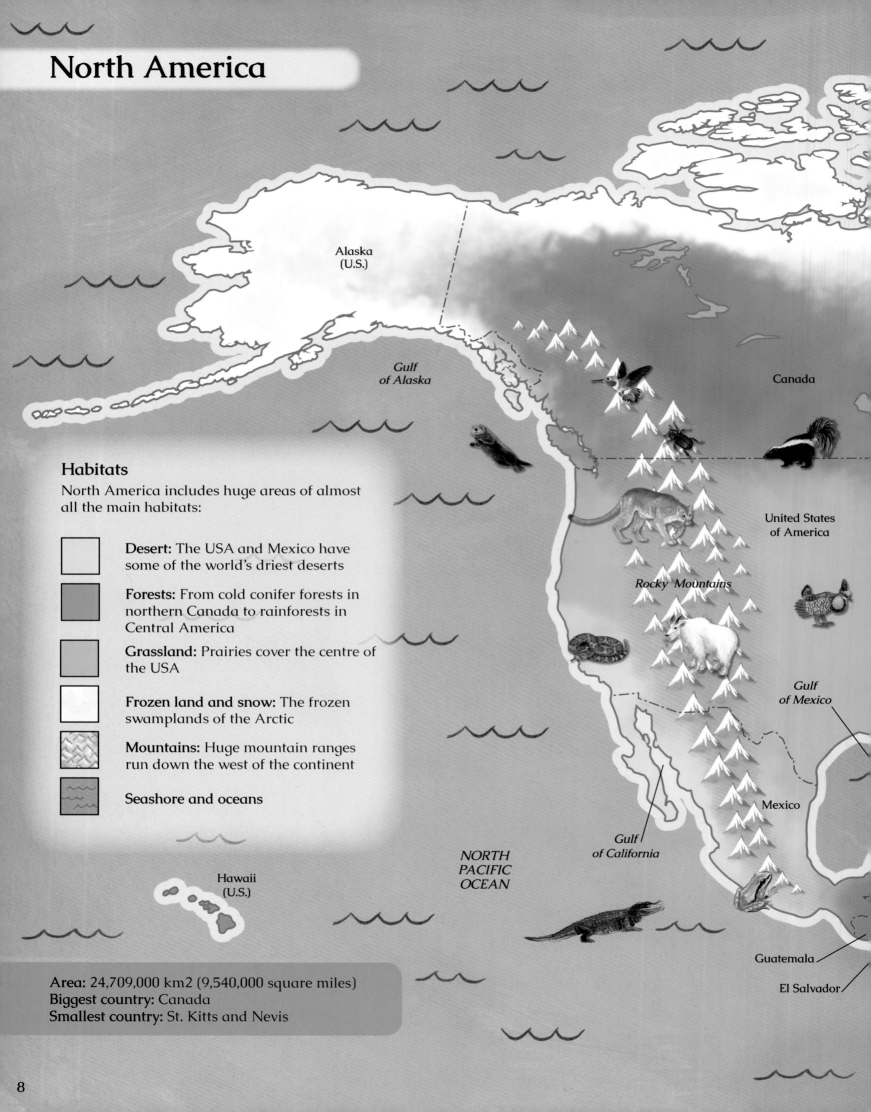

North America

Habitats

North America includes huge areas of almost all the main habitats:

Desert: The USA and Mexico have some of the world's driest deserts

Forests: From cold conifer forests in northern Canada to rainforests in Central America

Grassland: Prairies cover the centre of the USA

Frozen land and snow: The frozen swamplands of the Arctic

Mountains: Huge mountain ranges run down the west of the continent

Seashore and oceans

Area: 24,709,000 km2 (9,540,000 square miles)
Biggest country: Canada
Smallest country: St. Kitts and Nevis

Alaska
(U.S.)

Gulf
of Alaska

Hawaii
(U.S.)

NORTH
PACIFIC
OCEAN

Rocky Mountains

Canada

United States
of America

Gulf
of Mexico

Gulf
of California

Mexico

Guatemala

El Salvador

Greenland

Greenland
Sea

Baffin
Bay

Hudson
Bay

Mississipi
River

Appalachian
Mountains

The
Bahamas

Dominican
Republic

Puerto
Rico (U.S.)

Cuba

Haiti

Antigua and
Barbuda

Belize

St Lucia

Jamaica

St Vincent and
Grenadines

Barbados

Honduras

Caribbean
Sea

Grenada

Nicaragua

Costa Rica

Trinidad
and Tobago

Panama

NORTH
ATLANTIC
OCEAN

North America stretches from
the icy Arctic Circle in the
north to the steamy, sweltering
jungles of Costa Rica and
Panama in the south.
It's home to two of the world's
biggest countries, the USA
and Canada, as well as many
smaller nations. It has vast
areas of desert, forest, frozen
land and mountain wilderness,
where all kinds of amazing
animals roam.

Did you know?

In 2005, a rare millipede,
found only in central
California, USA, was
rediscovered after not being
seen for 80 years. It has
more legs than any other
animal – up to 750 of them!

9

North America:
Mountains, forests and the Pacific coast

The Rocky Mountains run all the way down the west side of North America (and also extend into South America, where they become the Andes). They form a massive mountain range with icy peaks that give way to rocky mountain meadows and evergreen mountain forests.

Humpback whale

The coast of eastern North America is a great place to spot humpback whales, as they migrate between their feeding areas around the Arctic, and their summer breeding areas near Hawaii or Mexico. Humpbacks are enormous, but so strong they can leap right out of the sea and splash back down – known as "breaching".

Pacific tree frog

The Pacific tree frog lives close to the coast of North America, from Mexico to Canada. It usually lives around ponds, like most frogs, but can also climb trees. Unlike most frogs, it really does say "ribbit!"

Sea otter

Sea otters live in the sea and on the shore around the northern Pacific. They dive to catch food such as clams and sea snails, then float on their backs to eat it.

Did you know?
Hummingbirds hover by beating their wings in a figure-of-8 pattern, up to 100 times per second, making a humming or buzzing sound.

Mountain goat

The white, woolly mountain goat is the biggest animal found in the high Rocky Mountains. Its sharp hooves and rubbery footpads give it such a good grip, it can climb and leap up steep, stony cliffs, where it looks for lichen, moss and small mountain plants to eat.

Mountain pine beetle

Shiny black pine beetles live in pine trees, like those in the conifer forests covering the Rocky Mountain slopes. They burrow under the bark and lay their eggs in the tree's wood. They are tiny – the size of a grain of rice – but they can damage and even kill the pine trees they nest in.

Rufous hummingbird

This little hummingbird spends the winter further south in Mexico or Florida, but in summer it flies north to the Rocky Mountains of the USA and Canada, even flying as far as Alaska.

11

North America: Prairies and deserts

Grasslands called prairies cover the middle part of North America, and large areas of them are now used for farmland, towns and cities. To the southwest it becomes hotter and drier, and the grassy meadows give way to the dusty deserts of the USA and Mexico.

Cougar

This powerful, long-legged big cat is one of the few North American animals that's been known to attack and eat humans! It often hides on a rocky ledge or up a tree, waiting for prey to pass by, then leaps down to pounce on it. Cougars can live in deserts, prairies and scrubland, as well as forests and mountains.

Greater prairie chicken

This odd-looking wild bird used to be common across North America's prairies, but is now rare due to hunting. To impress females, the males raise tufts of feathers over their heads and inflate bright orange pouches on their cheeks to make a call known as "booming".

Skunk

This small, stripy cat-like animal is famous for its unbearable stink, which it uses to defend itself. Skunks live throughout most of North America, in cities and in the countryside. They hide in burrows during the day, and come out at night to eat worms and insects, eggs, mushrooms and berries.

Black widow

Black widow spiders are widely feared, though they are actually not all that deadly, and rarely bite. They get their name because the female spiders sometimes eat the males. They live in the USA, Canada and Mexico.

Rattlesnake

Chrrrrrrr!! The dry, spooky sound of a rattlesnake shaking its tail is meant to scare you. It means this venomous snake is nearby, and could bite you if you bother it. Its deadly venom is horribly painful, and can even paralyse you.

North America:
Gulf coasts and Caribbean islands

To the south, North America narrows into an long isthmus, curving around a huge bay, the Gulf of Mexico. Its coast is dotted with sandy beaches, as well as swamps, marshlands and estuaries. Even further south is the warm Caribbean Sea, dotted with tropical islands.

Green sea turtle

The green sea turtle is found in oceans around the world, but females also come ashore to lay their eggs on sandy beaches. They wait until night-time to drag themselves up the beach and dig a nest in the sand.

West Indian manatee

This huge, slow-moving sea mammal likes to lounge in the warm, shallow waters around coasts and islands in the Caribbean Sea. It's a vegetarian, grazing on underwater sea grasses and plants. It comes to the surface every few minutes to breathe.

Bull shark

You might think that sharks only live in the sea, but the bull shark is an exception. It doesn't mind leaving salty seawater behind to swim into estuaries and up rivers, including the Mississippi in the USA, and the San Juan River in Nicaragua and Costa Rica.

Bald eagle

The bald eagle is the national bird of the USA, and also lives in Canada and Mexico. It's a huge bird of prey with a wingspan up to 2.3 metres across. It's not actually bald, though.

Did you know?
You can tell an alligator from a crocodile by its wide, rounded snout.

American alligator

There are only two types of alligators in the world – one lives in China, and the other, the American alligator, lives in the southern USA. It lurks in rivers and swampy wetlands, and can grow to be five metres (16 feet) long. As well as hunting fish, turtles and other water animals, alligators can catch and eat dogs, sheep, deer and even cows, when they come to the water to drink.

Saint Lucia parrot

Only found in the mountain forests of the small, lush Caribbean island of Saint Lucia, this national bird of Saint Lucia is incredibly noisy, known for its loud screeching, squawking and honking sounds.

South America

South America is a tall, triangle-shaped continent lying between the Atlantic and Pacific Oceans. In the north, it borders the tropical Caribbean. In the south, the chilly archipelago of Tierra del Fuego reaches almost to Antarctica. It's a land of remote jungles, mountains, deserts and huge, roaring rivers.

Area: 17,840,000 km2 (6,890,000 square miles)
Biggest country: Brazil
Smallest country: Suriname

SOUTH PACIFIC OCEAN

Did you know?
The Amazon rainforest is home to more different species of living things than any other land habitat in the world.

Pitcairn Islands

Habitats

Desert: The driest place in the world, the Atacama Desert, in South America

Forests: South America is famous for the huge rainforest around the River Amazon

Grassland: Including the northern savannah, the Argentinean Pampas and the far south

Mountains: Huge mountain ranges reach down the continent's western side

Seashore and oceans

Did you know?
In 2007, scientists exploring the Yariguies mountains, part of the Andes, discovered a previously unknown butterfly species. The summits of the Yariguies are so hard to reach, that instead of climbing them, the scientists had to drop down onto them from a helicopter.

16

Caribbean Sea

Venezuela

Suriname

Guyana

French Guiana (FR)

Colombia

Amazon River

Ecuador

Galapagos Islands

Peru

Andes

Brazil

Amazon Rainforest

Bolivia

The Atacama Desert

Paraguay

Chile

Andes

Uruguay

Argentina

The Pampas Plains

SOUTH ATLANTIC OCEAN

Patagonia

Glaciers of Patagonia

Falkland Islands

Archipelago of Tierra del Fuego

South America:
The Andes and the Amazon

The mighty Amazon River flows across the northern part of South America, surrounded by thick, damp tropical rainforest. Millions of trees, vines, plants, and a network of waterways are home to thousands of animal species. In the east, the jungle meets the huge icy-peaked Andes mountains, stretching 7,000 kilometres (4,350 miles) down the western side of South America.

Vicuna

Vicunas are related to camels, but are a lot smaller! Their wool is incredibly fine, soft and warm, but it can only be sheared once every few years, making it very expensive. The Inca people, who lived here hundreds of years ago, used vicuna wool. However, it was so precious only kings and queens were allowed to wear it.

Chinchilla

The chinchilla is a mountain rodent about the size of a rabbit. It has very thick fur which keeps it warm in the icy, windy Andes. Each of the hair follicles in its skin has up to 70 hairs growing from it (humans have only one or two!). Chinchillas are very good at jumping!

Red-bellied piranha

Piranhas are sharp-toothed river fish, famed for their fierce hunting habits and feeding frenzies. They mostly eat other fish. However, they do have a nasty bite and sometimes attack people. This species, the red-bellied piranha, is one of the biggest, at up to 33 centimetres (13 inches) long.

Spider monkey

Spider monkeys are perfectly adapted to rainforest life. They get their name from their long skinny limbs, and are brilliant climbers. Like other New World monkeys, they have prehensile tails that can curl and hold on to branches. Babies hitch a ride by hanging onto their mum's fur.

Andean condor

This giant vulture is an Andean condor, one of the world's biggest birds. It likes high, rocky mountainsides, where it can get a good view of the ground with its super-strength eyesight. It circles and swoops, looking out for its favourite food – the bodies of dead animals such as deer and vicunas.

Ocelot

The beautiful, sleek, spotted ocelot is a medium-sized wild cat found across most of South America, especially in jungles. It hunts at night, swimming and climbing, catching mice, birds, lizards and fish.

Brazilian wandering spider

If you see a spider like this waving its front legs in the air, run away! The Brazilian wandering spider gives this warning display when it's about to bite – and it has the deadliest bite of any spider in the world.

South America:
Patagonia and the Atacama

In the southern part of South America, steamy rainforests are replaced by drier habitats: the windy Pampas plains covered in long grass, the desert plateau and glaciers of the Patagonia mountains, and the bone-dry Atacama Desert. Some parts of this desert are so dry that nothing lives there at all!

Greater rhea

The rhea is a large flightless bird, with a bulky round body, long legs and a long neck, like an ostrich. It likes to hide in the long grass of the pampas, where it can stick its head up to look around, or lie down flat to hide from danger.

Grey gull

Once a year, these gulls leave their home on South America's Pacific coast and fly over 100 kilometres (60 miles) to the dry Atacama to lay their eggs. The male and female take turns to fly back to the sea for food. This is a clever way of keeping their eggs safe.

Southern elephant seal

Although not quite as big as a real elephant, a male southern elephant seal can grow to be as long and heavy as a small truck, with a massive, inflated snout. Patagonia is one of the areas where they come ashore to rest, breed and care for their babies on the icy or rocky beaches.

Did you know?
Armadillos can jump as much as one metre (three feet) straight up in the air when they're scared.

Grey zorro

This cute little dog-like mammal is also known as the chilla or South American grey fox. It lives throughout southern South America, except in the highest mountains, and eats mainly rabbits, birds and mice, as well as scorpions, armadillos, berries and bugs.

Pygmy armadillo

Armadillos are strange-looking creatures with a leathery, bendy shell. The pygmy armadillo or "pichi" is a small, hairy species that can survive in colder climates than other armadillos – partly by hibernating over the winter. It digs itself a burrow to live in, and can hide under its tough armour to avoid predators.

Atacama desert scorpion

Scorpions, which are related to spiders, are tough and well adapted to the extreme habitat of the desert, as they can survive on very little food and water. Scorpions like this one are among the very few animals found in the inhospitable Atacama Desert.

South America:
Galapagos Islands and hydrothermal vents

South America is home to some of the world's most exciting habitats, where scientists have been amazed to stumble across all kinds of bizarre creatures. The Galapagos Islands, situated off the coast of Ecuador, were made famous by Charles Darwin in the 1830s. Much more recently, in 1977, biologists discovered several new animal species living around hydrothermal (hot water) vents on the deep seabed nearby.

Vulcan octopus

Strange, pale, almost see-through, vulcan octopuses have been spotted around hydrothermal vents, preying on the vent crabs. They also feed on swarms of tiny shrimp-like animals, catching them by using the stretchy webbing between their arms like a fishing net.

Giant tube worm

These weird-looking worms can grow up to two metres (seven feet) long. They live around hydrothermal vents, where boiling hot water, full of dissolved minerals, flows out from under the seabed. They live inside hard tubes and reach out with their red, feathery plumes to collect chemicals from the water. They convert these chemicals into food.

Vent crab

Vent crabs are specially adapted to living around deep-sea hydrothermal vents. They hide among clusters of tube worms and feed on bacteria and larger sea creatures like mussels and clams. Their eyes can detect infrared and heat radiation, so they can see at night.

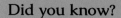
Blue-footed booby

The blue-footed booby gets its name
from its brightly coloured feet, and
from the Spanish word "bobo"
meaning fool or clown. On land, it
can look clumsy and silly, especially
when it lifts up its big blue feet and
shows them off to impress a mate.
But the booby is also a brilliant
hunter, flying from the cliffs and
plunging into the sea to catch fish
and squid.

Galapagos giant tortoise

The name "Galapagos" actually
means tortoise – Spanish explorers
named the islands after the giant
tortoises they found there.
They are rare today, having
been hunted for many years.
A giant tortoise's shell can
reach one and a half
metres long, and they
can live for up to
150 years!

Marine iguana

One animal you'll hardly
ever find in the sea is a
lizard. However in the
Galapagos there's one
exception – the frilly-
crested, dinosaur-like
marine iguana. They eat
sea algae (plant-like living things).
Seawater makes the iguanas freezing
cold, so after a dive they have to lie
on the rocks to warm up in the sun.

23

Africa

Africa is a huge, chunky, continent containing over 50 countries and more than a billion people. Its habitats range from baking deserts to thick, steamy jungles, towering volcanoes, tropical islands, and wide grassy plains where leopards, giraffes and wildebeest roam. The continent is close to the equator, and most of it lies in the tropics.

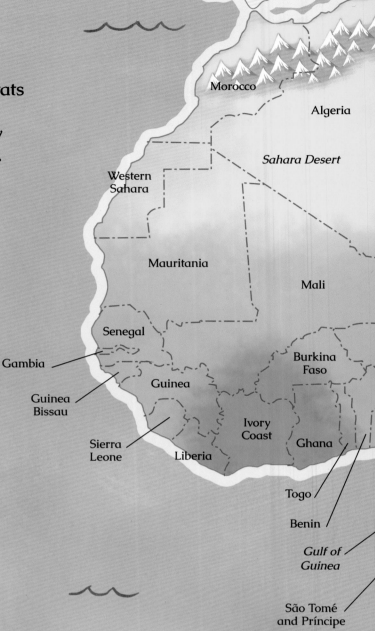

Morocco
Algeria
Sahara Desert
Western Sahara
Mauritania
Mali
Senegal
Gambia
Guinea
Burkina Faso
Guinea Bissau
Ivory Coast
Ghana
Sierra Leone
Liberia
Togo
Benin
Gulf of Guinea
São Tomé and Príncipe

Cape Verde

SOUTH ATLANTIC OCEAN

Area: 30,220,000 km2 (11,670,000 square miles)
Biggest country: Algeria
Smallest country: Seychelles

Habitats

Desert: Africa contains the Sahara, the world's biggest desert, plus several others

Forests: Central Africa's Congo basin is one of the world's biggest rainforest areas

Grassland: Grassy savannas dotted with trees cover much of the continent

Mountains: Africa has many mountains and mountain ranges, especially in the east

Seashore and oceans

Did you know?
The large island of Madagascar, off the coast of east Africa, is home to some amazing animals found nowhere else on Earth. They include the Madagascar moon moth, Parson's chameleon (the world's biggest chameleon), and over 50 different types of lemurs, furry animals related to monkeys.

Tunisia

Mediterranean
Sea

Libya

The Nile

Egypt

Red
Sea

Arabian
Sea

Niger

Chad

Sudan

Eritrea

Djibouti

Nigeria

Central
African Republic

South
Sudan

Somalia

Ethiopia

Cameroon

Equatorial
Guinea

Congo
Basin

Uganda

Kenya

Gabon

Congo

Congo
River

Democratic
Republic
of Congo

Rwanda

Lake
Victoria

Kilimanjaro

Seychelles

Burundi

Tanzania

Angola

Zambia

Malawi

Comoros

INDIAN
OCEAN

Okavango
Delta

Mozambique

Madagascar

Zimbabwe

Namibia

Botswana

Mauritius

Kalahari
Desert

Swaziland

Lesotho

South Africa

25

Africa:
Delta in the desert

A delta is a network of river channels and islands that forms where a river slows down and spreads out. Deltas are usually found where rivers join the sea. But in some places, a river can form a delta in the middle of the land. One is the Okavango Delta in Botswana, southern Africa, where the Okavango River flows into the hot, scrubby Kalahari Desert. Each year, after the rainy season, floods fill the delta, attracting wildlife from far around.

Boomslang

This unusual snake can be spotted in trees and bushes in the Okavango and surrounding desert, hunting chameleons and frogs. It can grow up to two metres (seven feet) long, and has a deadly bite. You can recognise it by its bright green colouring and extra-large, staring, pitch-black eyes.

Hippopotamus

The hippo, one of the world's biggest land animals, spends most of its day in water, coming out at night to feed on grass. They may seem slow and lumbering, but hippos are fierce, fast and can be very dangerous.

African catfish

Many fish in the Okavango have developed ways of surviving when the riverbeds dry up. African catfish are able to breathe in air as well as water, and can wriggle across land to find new water sources. They also bury themselves in mud in the dry season, to keep cool and damp until the water returns.

Gemsbok

The beautiful gemsbok is a large desert antelope. Gemsboks feed on grass and leaves, but in the dry season they also use their hooves to dig up roots to eat. They can manage without a drink of water for weeks on end, and can survive super-high temperatures.

Ostrich

This amazing giant bird stands up to 50 per cent taller than an adult human. It can't fly, but is a very fast runner, and sometimes chases and kicks other animals that annoy it. Its long neck and sharp eyesight give it a brilliant long-distance view, so it can look out for danger and spot plants to eat.

Cheetah

Cheetahs are spotty big cats known for their high-speed running skills. As well as living in grasslands, they are good at surviving in deserts, where they hunt antelopes like gemsboks and springboks. When water is in short supply, cheetahs get a drink by eating the juicy melons that grow in the desert.

Africa:
Rivers and rainforests of the Congo

Like rainforests around the world, the rainforest in central Africa is being chopped down for timber and farmland. What's left is hugely important for wildlife. This forest contains some of the most fascinating, rare and shy animal species in the world, including chimpanzees, our closest relatives. Through the rainforest runs the mighty Congo River, filled with unusual fish and wild water creatures.

Common or Eurasian cuckoo

The common cuckoo migrates to Europe or Asia in the spring, but in the chilly northern winters it can be found here, deep in the Congo rainforest. It's famous for laying its eggs in other birds' nests, so its chicks can be fed and raised by them.

Nile crocodile

The Nile crocodile is one of the world's largest and most dangerous crocodiles, and lives not only in the Nile, but also in the Congo and many other rivers across Africa. They lurk in the water, snapping up fish and also grabbing larger animals from the riverbank.

Longnose elephant fish

A small, strange-looking and very rare fish, the longnose elephant fish uses its long snout to snuffle through the mud on the riverbed, feeling for insects.

Chimpanzee

Chimpanzees are highly intelligent, endangered forest apes that live in large groups. They were once thought to be mild-mannered vegetarians, but we now know that chimps go hunting, fight wars against each other, can communicate with calls and facial expressions, and use tools – for example, using sharp stones to chop up food.

Did you know?

Victorian English explorer Mary Kingsley visited the Congo basin in the 1890s, encountering many wild animals. Once a crocodile climbed on to her canoe! Luckily, she gave him a "clip on the snout with a paddle" and he went away.

Straw-coloured fruit bat

These very big fruit bats with large ears and long, pointy noses are found in colonies of up to 10 million bats. The colonies migrate to feed on different types of fruit as they ripen. In parts of Zambia, tourists gather to see the skies darken with millions of bats flying overhead.

Army ants

Also called safari ants, driver ants or "siafu", these ants live in enormous groups or colonies numbering up to 20 million in one colony alone. When food runs short, a colony may go on the march, surging through the jungle in a massive swarm, and devouring any animal in its path.

Africa:
Grasslands and highlands

Eastern Africa is a land of savannas, high plateaus and mountains. This is the home of Africa's most famous wildlife parks, such as the Serengeti, Ngorongoro and Maasai Mara, where millions of tourists go in the hope of spotting lions, elephants, giraffes and wildebeest. The mountains are home to many amazing animals too, such as wolves and the mountain gorilla.

Lion

The lion isn't really the king of the jungle, as lions don't live in jungles! They like grassy savannas dotted with a few trees to let them hide and sneak up on antelopes, zebras and other prey. Males look impressive with their thick, furry manes, but female lions actually do the most hunting.

African elephant

The biggest land animal on Earth, a large male can stand up to four metres (13 feet) tall, with a two metre (6.5 feet) long trunk and ears the size of sofas. Elephants roam the savannas in family groups, led by an older female, who guards her family fiercely.

Malachite sunbird

Sunbirds are small birds that feed on insects and flower nectar. While females are brownish, males often have colourful, iridescent feathers. The beautiful green and blue malachite sunbird can be spotted on the slopes of Africa's highest mountain, Kilimanjaro in Tanzania, and in other hilly areas.

Mountain gorilla

Shy, vegetarian and extremely rare, mountain gorillas can be hard to see as they lounge among thick vegetation high in the volcanic Virunga mountains, munching on leaves. They spend most of the day eating, and sleep in a newly-built leafy nest every night.

Ethiopian wolf

This small, marmalade-coloured wolf is Africa's only wolf species, and is seriously endangered. It lives on the high moorlands of Ethiopia, more than 3,000 metres (10,000 feet) above sea level, hunting small mountain rodents such as mole rats.

Did you know?

Mountain gorillas hate getting wet! They hide from rain and stay away from rivers and streams, only crossing them if there are logs or stones to step on.

Giant African millipede

Looking like a shiny, rubbery tube, the giant millipede shuffles and wriggles through fallen leaves and dead plants, feeding on rotting fruit and other plant matter. Although "millipede" means 1,000 legs, this one has only around 300. It can grow to be 35 centimetres (14 inches) long and as thick as a banana.

Europe

Europe is part of an enormous land mass known as Eurasia, and is connected to Asia in the east. Europe reaches from the icy Arctic Ocean in the north to the warmer coasts of the Mediterranean, Black and Caspian Seas. Though it's a small continent, only a third as big as Africa, its coastline is much longer, due to its many inlets and islands. Besides its coastal habitats, Europe includes lots of forests, moorlands and mountains – but much of its land has now been turned into farmland and cities.

ARCTIC OCEAN

Iceland

Norwegian Sea

Habitats

Europe is mainly temperate in climate – neither very hot nor very cold. It features large areas of these habitats:

Forests: In its natural state, most of Europe was covered in forests. Conifer forests reach across Europe's chilly northern areas

Grassland: Where Europe approaches Asia, grassy plains called steppes dominate

Mountains: Europe's impressive mountain ranges include the Alps, Pyrenees and Caucasus, and the volcanoes of Greece, Italy and Iceland

Frozen land and snow: Frozen landscapes lie in the chilly far north

Seashore and oceans

Did you know?

The Caspian Sea was once linked to the world's other seas and oceans, but became cut off in prehistoric times so now it is more like a giant, slightly salty lake. It's home to some creatures found nowhere else on Earth, such as the Caspian seal, the world's smallest seal species.

Norway

North Sea

Denmark

Northern Ireland

Ireland

United Kingdom

Netherlands

German

Belgium

Luxembourg

Liech

France

Switzerland

Alps

Monaco

Pyrenees

Andorra

Mediterranean Sea

NORTH ATLANTIC OCEAN

Bay of Biscay

Portugal

Spain

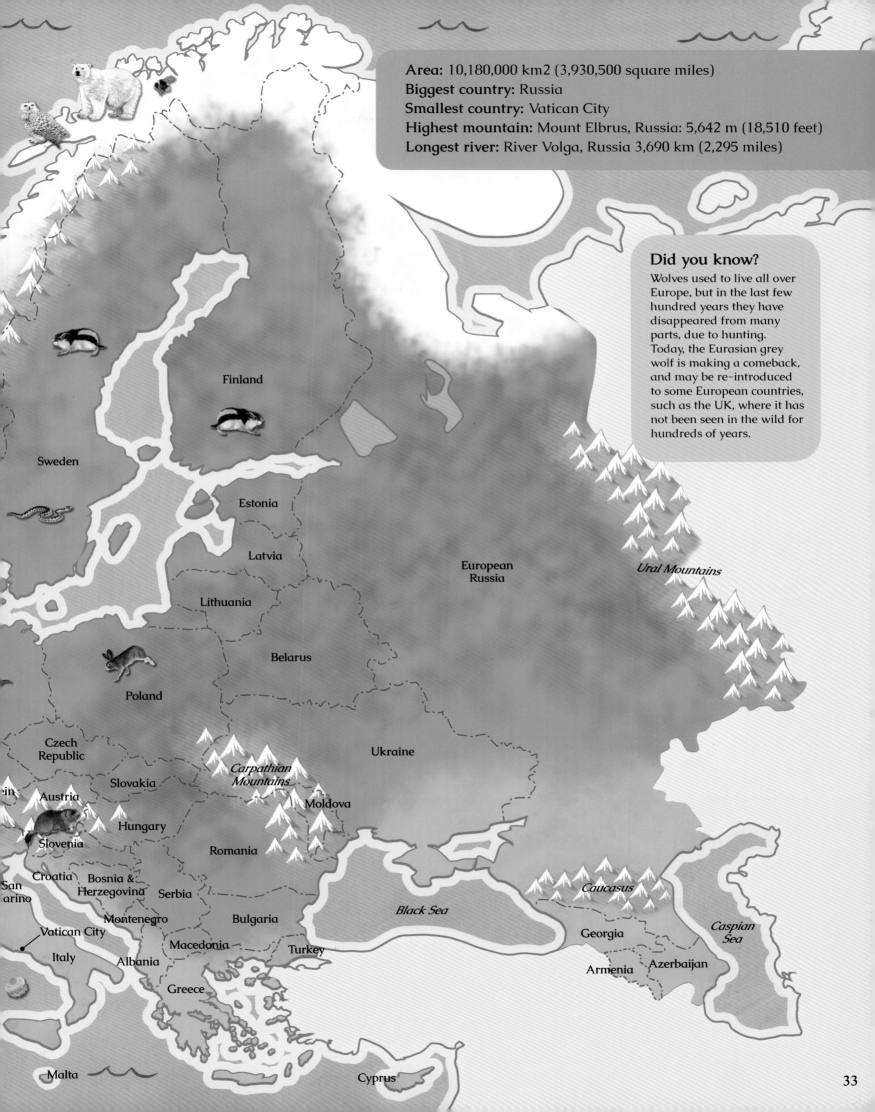

Area: 10,180,000 km2 (3,930,500 square miles)
Biggest country: Russia
Smallest country: Vatican City
Highest mountain: Mount Elbrus, Russia: 5,642 m (18,510 feet)
Longest river: River Volga, Russia 3,690 km (2,295 miles)

Did you know?

Wolves used to live all over Europe, but in the last few hundred years they have disappeared from many parts, due to hunting. Today, the Eurasian grey wolf is making a comeback, and may be re-introduced to some European countries, such as the UK, where it has not been seen in the wild for hundreds of years.

Finland

Sweden

Estonia

Latvia

Ural Mountains

Lithuania

European Russia

Belarus

Poland

Czech Republic

Ukraine

Slovakia

Carpathian Mountains

ein

Austria

Moldova

Hungary

Slovenia

Romania

Caucasus

Croatia

Bosnia & Herzegovina

San arino

Serbia

Black Sea

Caspian Sea

Montenegro

Bulgaria

Georgia

Vatican City

Macedonia

Italy

Turkey

Azerbaijan

Albania

Armenia

Greece

Malta

Cyprus

Europe:
From the mountains to the Mediterranean

The Alps are Europe's biggest mountain range, with lots of snowy peaks and frozen glaciers, and their own mountain ecosystems and animals. These mighty mountains lie close to the Mediterranean Sea, the southern border of Europe. Its coasts feature the dry, warm, bushy climate known as the Mediterranean habitat, while its warm waters are home to many kinds of sea creatures. Many of the animals shown here can be found in other areas of Europe.

Wild boar

Where the Alps approach the coast, wild boar can be found living in the forests and bushy, scrubby Mediterranean landscape. They are big, fierce wild pigs with four long, sharp tusks, used for fighting and defending themselves.

Mountain Apollo butterfly

The beautiful white Apollo butterfly lives on mountainsides where there's a mixture of grassy flower meadows and bare, rocky slopes. The adults feed on nectar from the flowers, while the caterpillars eat plants called stonecrop and houseleek, which grow among the stones.

Large Alpine salamander

This big, black salamander was only discovered in 1988, living in mountain meadows in the south-western Alps. Salamanders are amphibians, like frogs and toads, but the large Alpine salamander is unusual – it prefers to live in the grassy meadows rather than near water.

Short-beaked common dolphin

Common dolphins can often be spotted following boats on the Mediterranean. They swim fast, close to the water surface, and often splash, play and leap in and out of the waves. You can spot them by the criss-cross markings on their sides, short, stubby snouts and cream-coloured bellies.

Alpine marmot

Marmots are big, fat and fluffy squirrel-like animals that live on high mountain slopes all over Europe. All summer, they feed themselves up on grass, seeds and flowers. Then they spend the long winter hibernating in their burrows.

Fried egg jellyfish

This bizarre-looking jellyfish has short tentacles and a smooth, white and yellow dome on top, so it really does look like a fried egg. It can grow to 50 centimetres (20 inches) across, as big as a dustbin lid, but doesn't have a dangerous sting.

Europe:
Scottish moorland, sea cliffs and seashore

Scotland is the most northerly part of the United Kingdom, and one of the wilder corners of Europe. It's quite small, but has some amazing areas of mountain, moor and island wilderness that make a great home for wildlife.

Gannet
Scotland's sea cliffs and rocky islands are home to huge numbers of these stunning seabirds. They nest on rocky ledges, and plunge into the sea at an astonishing speed to grab fish from deep under the water. Gannets are big and powerful, with a wingspan of up to almost two metres (six feet) wide.

Atlantic salmon
Salmon spend most of their lives out at sea. When they are ready to breed, they swim up rivers until they reach shallow streams where they lay their eggs. The young salmon eventually head back to sea, and later return to the place where they were born to lay their own eggs.

Did you know?
Scotland is home to the adder and the grass snake, but Ireland, its close neighbour, has no snakes at all.

Red deer

A large red deer stag can be a breathtaking sight, with his enormous branched antlers spreading up to a metre (three feet) across. The stags use their antlers to charge and wrestle with each other as a way of fighting over female deer, sometimes even killing each other.

Red grouse

The red grouse is a typical Scottish animal. It lives on moorlands covered with heather and small bushes, giving the birds a place to hide from predators. Red grouse have feathers all the way down their legs and even on their feet and toes, to help them keep warm in the winter.

Common adder

Adders are snakes that can live on high mountains and moorlands, forests, marshes and sand dunes close to the sea. They survive the winter by hibernating. Adders have a poisonous bite, used for killing mice, lizards and other prey.

Mountain hare

Mountain hares are brown in the summer, but their fur turns white during the winter, to camouflage them against the snowy moors and mountains. They also have very large, furry feet to help them walk over the snow without sinking into it.

Europe:
Arctic tundra and the Arctic Ocean

The tundra habitat is made up of soggy, marshy soil that's mostly or partly frozen. It's found around the poles, where the climate is cold and summers are short. Few trees can survive, but there are mosses, lichens and flowering plants that support animals like small rodents and insects, which larger animals hunt. In Europe, tundra is found in northern Norway and Russia, close to the icy Arctic Ocean.

Polar bear

Norway's northern coasts and islands, and the sea ice around them, are also home to the mighty polar bear. The polar bear is the biggest carnivore on the planet. Polar bears wander across frozen seas, or swim from one ice shelf to another, to hunt for seals. Female bears make burrows in the snow or soil, where they give birth to and shelter their cubs.

Arctic tern

Each year, Arctic terns fly all the way from the North Pole to the South Pole and back again – an incredible distance of 40,000 kilometres (25,000 miles) – so that they can spend the summer in both places. Though small, they are fierce, and will dive-bomb anyone who gets too close to their nests.

Greenland shark

Below the icy waters off Europe's northern coast lurks the gigantic Greenland shark. It's one of the world's biggest sharks, reaching up to seven metres (23 feet) long. It lives in the deep sea, but sometimes swims up to shallower water near the coast to keep warm during winter. It eats any food it can find, including reindeer and horses that happen to venture into the sea!

Snowy owl

The beautiful snowy owl can be pure white, or speckled with darker spots. It makes its nest on the tundra and goes hunting during the day, catching small animals like lemmings, fish, or birds. One snowy owl can catch over a thousand lemmings in a year!

Norway lemming

Lemmings are small, furry rodents. The Norway lemming feeds on moss and other small plants. In winter, these lemmings dig pathways and hollows underneath the deep snow, where they can keep warm and find food.

Arctic bumblebee

As small animals like insects lose heat easily, not many live in freezing cold places. Arctic bumblebee queens survive by spending most of the year sheltering underground, then come out in the summer to breed a small colony of worker bees. These bees can also use vibrations of their flight muscles to warm up their bodies.

Asia

Asia is a huge continent, the world's biggest. It stretches from the Arabian deserts in the west to the far eastern islands of Japan, the Philippines and Indonesia; from icy Siberia in the north to Indonesia's tropical coral reefs. Its countries, including giants like Russia, India and China, are spread across a vast continental land mass surrounded by many thousands of islands. Asia is known for its mighty Himalayan mountain range, as well as its tropical reefs, beaches and rainforests.

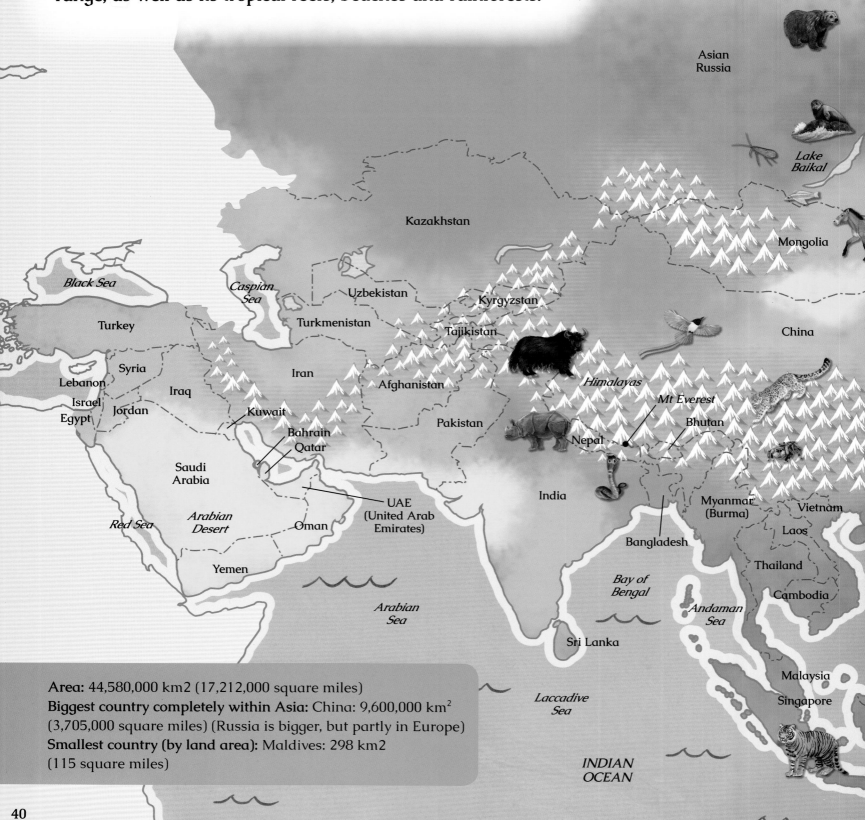

Asian Russia

Lake Baikal

Kazakhstan

Mongolia

Black Sea

Caspian Sea

Uzbekistan

Kyrgyzstan

China

Turkey

Turkmenistan

Tajikistan

Syria

Iran

Himalayas

Lebanon

Iraq

Afghanistan

Mt Everest

Israel

Jordan

Kuwait

Bhutan

Egypt

Bahrain

Nepal

Qatar

Pakistan

Saudi Arabia

India

UAE (United Arab Emirates)

Myanmar (Burma)

Vietnam

Red Sea

Arabian Desert

Oman

Laos

Bangladesh

Thailand

Yemen

Bay of Bengal

Cambodia

Arabian Sea

Andaman Sea

Sri Lanka

Malaysia

Laccadive Sea

Singapore

Area: 44,580,000 km2 (17,212,000 square miles)
Biggest country completely within Asia: China: 9,600,000 km² (3,705,000 square miles) (Russia is bigger, but partly in Europe)
Smallest country (by land area): Maldives: 298 km2 (115 square miles)

INDIAN OCEAN

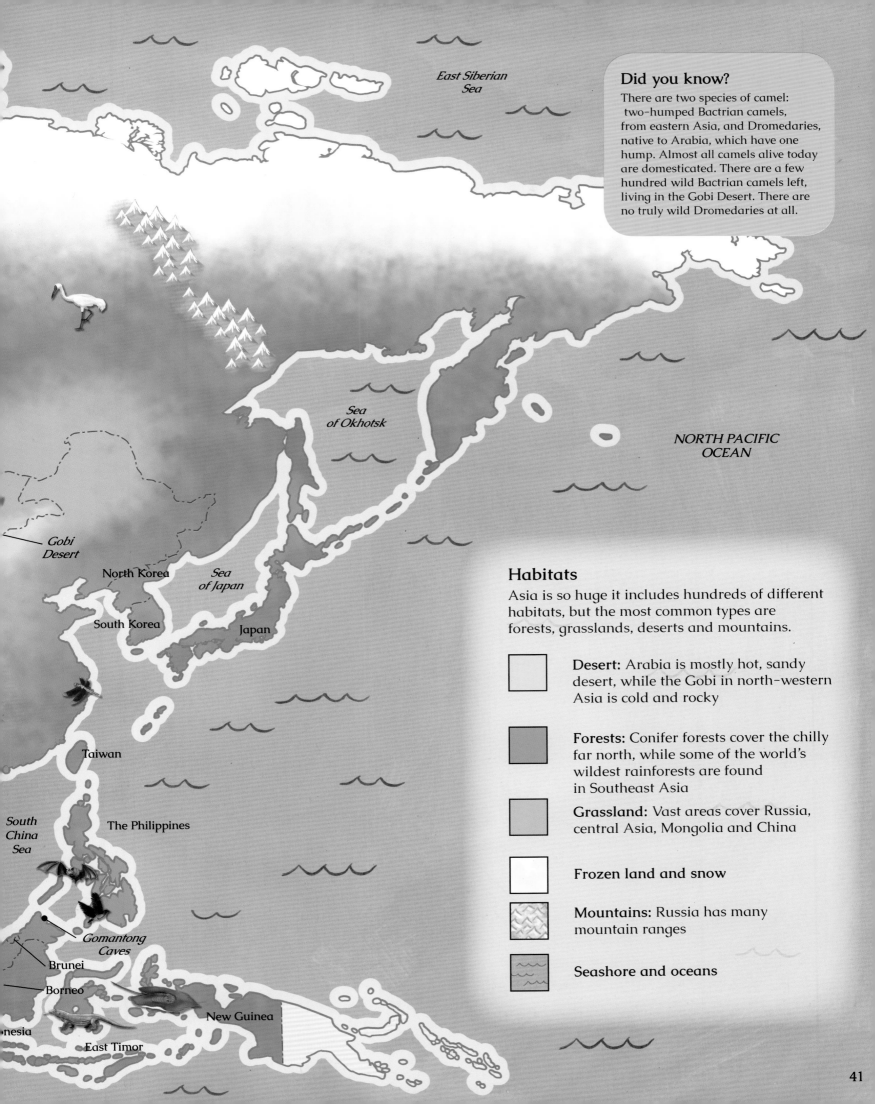

East Siberian
Sea

Did you know?
There are two species of camel:
two-humped Bactrian camels,
from eastern Asia, and Dromedaries,
native to Arabia, which have one
hump. Almost all camels alive today
are domesticated. There are a few
hundred wild Bactrian camels left,
living in the Gobi Desert. There are
no truly wild Dromedaries at all.

Sea
of Okhotsk

NORTH PACIFIC
OCEAN

*Gobi
Desert*

North Korea

Sea
of Japan

South Korea

Japan

Habitats

Asia is so huge it includes hundreds of different
habitats, but the most common types are
forests, grasslands, deserts and mountains.

Desert: Arabia is mostly hot, sandy
desert, while the Gobi in north-western
Asia is cold and rocky

Forests: Conifer forests cover the chilly
far north, while some of the world's
wildest rainforests are found
in Southeast Asia

Grassland: Vast areas cover Russia,
central Asia, Mongolia and China

Frozen land and snow

Mountains: Russia has many
mountain ranges

Seashore and oceans

Taiwan

South
China
Sea

The Philippines

*Gomantong
Caves*

Brunei

Borneo

New Guinea

nesia

East Timor

Asia:
High Himalayas to lowland swamps

The Himalayas, in the middle of Asia, are the highest mountains in the world. Some soar to over 8,000 metres above sea level, which is as high as aeroplanes fly. Their icy peaks have little wildlife, but lower down live tough mountain animals that can survive the wind and cold. The high Himalayas are surrounded by smaller foothills, leading down to grasslands and swamps.

Himalayan paradise flycatcher

The beautiful paradise flycatcher, with its long trailing tail feathers, is a common bird across most of Asia. There are several different types or subspecies, with different colours. The Himalayan type is orange with a white chest and blue-black head. It can be spotted in forests in the Himalayan foothills, darting about to snatch insects from the air.

Spectacled cobra

Growing up to two and a half metres long, you can tell this large and deadly snake by the spectacle-shaped marking on the back of its neck, which it spreads out into a wide "hood" when threatened. There are also two black markings on the front of its neck.

Indian rhino

Also called the greater one-horned rhino, this huge, heavy rhinoceros is found in the swampy lowlands of India and Nepal. It feeds on tall grasses and fruits, and loves wallowing in the waterways and muddy marshes.

Snow leopard

Among the rocky, snowy slopes of the high Himalayas lurks a very big cat – the very rare, super-furry snow leopard. Its silvery-beige spotted coat gives it great camouflage so it can sneak up on mountain sheep and goats – and also makes it very hard for humans to spot.

Wild yak

The biggest animal in the Himalayas is the wild yak, a horned, hairy mammal related to cows. Males can be three metres long, with horns measuring over 90 centimetres (three feet). The yak's thick, shaggy coat reaches almost to the ground.

Himalayan jumping spider

This amazing spider is tiny but tough. It's no bigger than your fingertip, but can survive 6,500 metres up in the rocky Himalayan slopes – making it one of the highest-dwelling animals in the world. Like other jumping spiders, it can see brilliantly with its eight eyes, and catches prey by pouncing on it.

Did you know?

Poachers (illegal hunters) kill rhinos to take their horns, which are wrongly thought to be a powerful medicine.

Asia:
Siberia and Lake Baikal

Lake Baikal is the deepest and oldest lake on the planet. It lies in chilly Siberia, part of Russia, and freezes over every winter. At its deepest point, it is 1,640 metres to the bottom – so deep, it could hold ten 60-storey skyscrapers stacked on top of each other! The lake is also home to hundreds of unique creatures that are found nowhere else in the world.

Baikal seal

This small, beautiful seal is also known as the "nerpa". It's very unusual for a seal to live in a freshwater lake – most seals live in the salty oceans. Scientists still don't know how seals ended up in Lake Baikal, so far away from the sea. By night, nerpas dive 100 metres below the lake surface to feast on their favourite food, the golomyanka fish.

Golomyanka

The golomyanka is only found in Lake Baikal. It's also called the "oilfish" or "fatfish", as almost 40 per cent of its body is made up of oil – making it a great high-energy food for seals and other animals.

Caddis fly

Caddis flies are large, moth-like flies. Their larvae, or young, live under the water. They build themselves a shell by gluing stones, twigs, shells or sand around their bodies with sticky silk. In springtime, they become flying adults, and millions of them emerge from the water to lay their eggs.

Siberian brown bear

Brown bears live in many parts of the world, including in the mountains around Lake Baikal. In spring and early summer, they come down to the lake's shores to feed on the swarms of caddis flies. Bears are known as fierce hunters, but they also love eating insects, berries, eggs and honey.

Przewalski's horse

Most "wild" horses are farm animals that have escaped and become feral. The Przewalski's horse is the only true wild horse, and shows how horses looked thousands of years ago before humans began to tame and breed them. At one time, these horses died out in the wild, but they survived in zoos and have now been re-introduced to the steppes of Mongolia, south of Lake Baikal.

Siberian crane

The Siberian crane stands almost as tall as a human, and has pure white feathers, black wingtips and a red beak and leathery "mask" on its face. It lives in boggy, watery areas where it can eat plants, fish and frogs.

Asia:
Island jungles and giant caves

Southeast Asia is made up of lots of peninsulas and islands. For example, the nation of Indonesia alone has at least 18,000 islands! They range from big islands like Sumatra, Java and Borneo to tiny tropical atolls in the sea. This part of Asia has a lot of rainforests, especially the island of Borneo, shared by Indonesia and Malaysia, which is also home to the Gomantong cave system and its unusual wildlife.

Komodo dragon

The world's largest lizard lives on just three small islands in Indonesia. It's a chunky, dinosaur-like beast, measuring up to three metres (10 feet), including its huge tail. It can kill and eat animals as large as goats, cows and even humans. Komodos are famous for dribbling and drooling, and their slimy saliva contains deadly bacteria and venom.

Giant freshwater stingray

Look at this monster! It's a massive stingray and it's one of the biggest freshwater fish on the planet. It lives in slow-flowing jungle rivers and estuaries in Borneo, New Guinea and other parts of Southeast Asia. A large giant stingray can reach up to 2.4 metres (eight feet) long.

Wrinkle-lipped bat

Millions of wrinkle-lipped bats roost or settle in the Gomantong caves during the daytime, then fly out in huge swarms at dusk to go hunting for flying insects. Inside the caves there are enormous heaps of horrendously smelly bat guano, or droppings, where cockroaches and other insects lay their eggs.

Did you know?

Wrinkle-lipped bat guano is also useful for humans – they collect it to use as a fertilizer for crops.

Edible-nest swiftlet

Cave swiftlets are small birds that make their nests in caves. Their nests are actually made out of their own saliva, hardened and glued onto the cave walls. The edible-nest swiftlet gets its name because people collect the nests and use them to make a type of soup.

Red grasshawk

The red grasshawk is a striking red dragonfly that's common across Southeast Asia. It's also called the "common parasol" or "flame skimmer". Grasshawks aren't shy, and often dart and flutter around people. However they tend to stay close to water, where they lay their eggs and hunt other flying insects.

Sumatran tiger

The Sumatran tiger is found in the wild only on Sumatra, one of Indonesia's main islands. It's the smallest of the five subspecies of tiger surviving today, and it's very endangered. It prowls the tropical jungles, hunting wild deer and pigs.

Oceania

Palau

Micronesia

Bismarck Sea

Solomon Islands

Papua New Guinea

Solomon Sea

Arafura Sea

Christmas Island (AUS)

Timor Sea

Coral Sea

INDIAN OCEAN

Australia

Great Divider Range

Great Australian Bight

To the south and east of Asia lie the enormous island nation of Australia, and many smaller islands and archipelagos spreading across the Pacific Ocean. This part of the world is known as Oceania, Australia/Oceania, or sometimes Australasia. It's home to a variety of fascinating and unusual animals that have developed in isolation, separately from the rest of the world's wildlife.

Tasmania

Tasman Sea

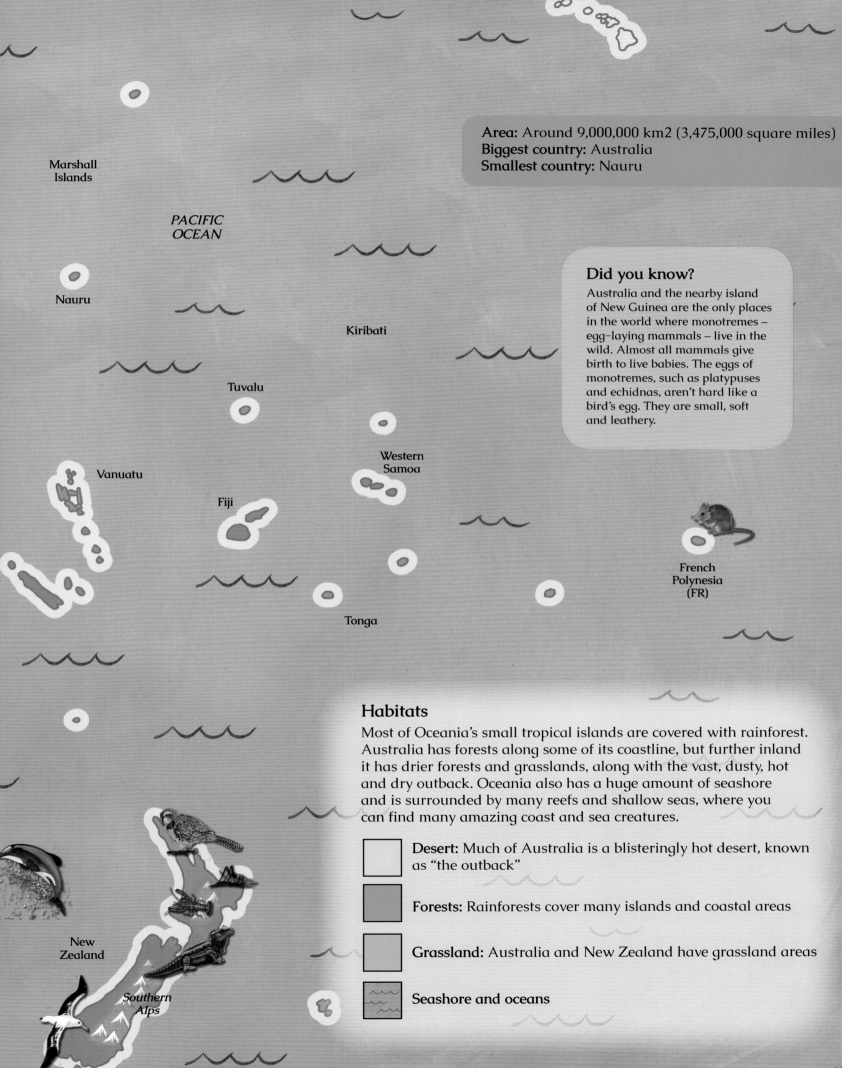

Marshall
Islands

*PACIFIC
OCEAN*

Nauru

Kiribati

Tuvalu

Western
Samoa

Vanuatu

Fiji

Tonga

French
Polynesia
(FR)

New
Zealand

*Southern
Alps*

Area: Around 9,000,000 km2 (3,475,000 square miles)
Biggest country: Australia
Smallest country: Nauru

Did you know?

Australia and the nearby island of New Guinea are the only places in the world where monotremes – egg-laying mammals – live in the wild. Almost all mammals give birth to live babies. The eggs of monotremes, such as platypuses and echidnas, aren't hard like a bird's egg. They are small, soft and leathery.

Habitats

Most of Oceania's small tropical islands are covered with rainforest. Australia has forests along some of its coastline, but further inland it has drier forests and grasslands, along with the vast, dusty, hot and dry outback. Oceania also has a huge amount of seashore and is surrounded by many reefs and shallow seas, where you can find many amazing coast and sea creatures.

Desert: Much of Australia is a blisteringly hot desert, known as "the outback"

Forests: Rainforests cover many islands and coastal areas

Grassland: Australia and New Zealand have grassland areas

Seashore and oceans

Oceania:

Australia's outback, forests and coasts

Australia is a huge island landmass, so big it can be counted as a continent all by itself. It has a thick, bean-like shape and its inner area, far from the sea, is very hot and dry. This scrubby, sandy desert land, called the outback, is home to animals not found anywhere else on Earth, such as kangaroos. Nearer the sea, Australia can be cooler and damper, with wildlife-filled rainforests, rivers and streams, leading to warm tropical ocean shores.

Giant burrowing frog

This big, brown, bumpy-skinned frog lives in burrows near freshwater in coastal parts of southeast Australia. Its eyes are very large, and so are its chunky, slow-swimming tadpoles when they hatch out of their eggs. The giant burrowing frog is also called the "owl frog", as its mating call is a spooky, owl-like hooting sound.

Southern blue-ringed octopus

This small, but dangerous octopus is found in rock pools along Australia's coast. It's usually pale brown, but like other octopuses, it can change colour. When it flashes its bright blue ring markings on a vivid yellow background, this means it's about to bite. Its deadly venom can kill a human in minutes.

Red kangaroo

Australia is the home of several species of kangaroo and their relatives such as wallabies. The red kangaroo is the biggest and is roughly as tall as a fully grown man. Kangaroos get around by jumping on their big back legs, and can leap an amazing eight to nine metres (26 to 29 feet) with each bound.

Koala

Koalas look like cute, cuddly teddy bears. However, they have sharp claws, and can scratch and bite to defend themselves. They live in and feed on eucalyptus trees. They hardly ever need to leave the trees, as they get all the water they need from the leaves, and sleep wedged into gaps between the branches.

Inland taipan

This desert snake is thought to be the most venomous snake in the world. The venom in a single bite could kill 100 people! Because of this, it's also known as the "fierce snake". However, it's actually very shy, and hardly ever attacks people, feeding instead on desert mice and birds.

Platypus

The platypus has a beak and webbed feet like a duck, a wide beaver-like tail, and a sleek body designed for swimming. Males also have poisonous spines on their back feet. Platypuses are river animals, diving to catch water worms and snails by night, and sheltering in riverbank burrows by day.

Oceania:
New Zealand

Many people in other parts of the world think Australia and New Zealand are close neighbours. In fact, they're over 2,000 kilometres (1,250 miles) apart, and New Zealand has its own unique landscape and climate. Its two main islands and many of its smaller ones have high mountains, volcanoes, hot springs, caves and forests where you can find unusual birds, lizards and creepy-crawlies. New Zealand's shores and seas are also home to some unique animal species.

Tuatara

This dragon-like reptile looks like a lizard, but isn't. The two species of tuatara form their own special reptile group, and their only relatives are long-extinct prehistoric creatures. Unusually for reptiles, tuataras like cold weather. They move very slowly, have long lives (possibly up to a hundred years), and their eggs take a whole year to hatch.

Hector's dolphin

Hector's dolphins only live around the coast of New Zealand, where they hunt fish and squid. They're the smallest of all sea dolphins and are rare and endangered. You can spot a Hector's dolphin by its pale grey back, curved black markings on its face, and its unusual dorsal fin, which is round instead of pointed.

Southern royal albatross

Albatrosses are big seabirds with a very wide wingspan. They spend most of their time soaring over the sea, plucking fish and squid from the water. The Southern royal albatross can be seen at sea in many parts of the Southern Ocean surrounding Antarctica, but it lands on New Zealand to nest and breed.

Kakapo

The kakapo is a forest parrot only found in New Zealand. It's the world's biggest and heaviest parrot, and cannot fly. When settlers brought animals like cats and dogs from other countries, they could easily hunt kakapos, which soon became very rare. Today, the few remaining kakapos have been moved to safe nature reserves.

Cave Weta

Wetas are cricket-like insects that can grow to a scarily huge size. There are many types in New Zealand, including giant wetas, which are among the world's heaviest insects. Cave wetas lurk in caves, mines and cellars and can give you a fright when they suddenly hop into the air.

Koura

Kouras, also known as "crawlies", are freshwater crayfish. They live in streams and lakes, and are related to sea creatures like crabs and lobsters. They eat old, dead leaves and insects that fall to the bottom of the water. If a koura is alarmed, it will flick its tail suddenly, making it shoot backwards.

Oceania:
Pacific islands, reefs and sea life

The islands of Oceania are home to all kinds of forest, seashore and ocean life. Around the islands there are a lot of coral reefs – large structures formed in the sea by tiny animals called coral polyps. Some of the islands themselves are also built from coral. Coral reefs provide a home and food for a huge variety of sea creatures.

Did you know?
Coral reefs are the biggest structures on Earth that have been created by animals – far bigger than anything humans have built.

Giant clam

While diving among the Pacific's colourful coral reefs, you could come across the owner of the biggest seashell in the world – a giant clam. Its ginormous shell can measure 1.2 metres (four feet) wide, and is fixed to the coral, so the clam can't move around. It lives on plankton, and food made by tiny algae (plant-like creatures) that live inside it. Despite their size, giant clams do not eat larger animals, and do not snap shut and grab people by the leg!

Coral polyps

Coral polyps are small, simple sea creatures. Their bodies are soft and squishy, but they build a hard shell or skeleton around themselves, just as many other sea animals do. Coral polyps often live in groups or colonies. As old polyps die and new ones grow, more and more layers of coral skeletons are built up – and over time, this forms huge coral reefs.

Great hammerhead

Prowling around the reefs is another monster of the shallow seas, the great hammerhead shark, which can grow to six metres (20 feet) long. It hunts other animals that live on coral reefs, such as crabs and lobsters, squid and stingrays. Its oddly-shaped head, with the eyes set far apart on each end, is thought to help it scan the seabed for prey.

Coral which is made up of coral polyps

Giant clam

Superb bird of paradise

The strange creature in this picture hardly looks like a bird at all! It's actually a male superb bird of paradise from Papua New Guinea, doing his mating display to impress a female. Most of the time, he looks like a glossy blue and black crow, but to display, he arranges his feathers into a wide fan shape, hops about and makes a clicking noise.

Polynesian rat

Rats have spread all over the world, and in the Pacific islands, the Polynesian rat is the most common. It is thought to have spread across the Pacific with humans, hitching a ride on their boats. It's a small rat that's very good at climbing and can eat almost any food.

Christmas Island red crab

Christmas Island is a small island belonging to Australia, and is the only place in the world where the Christmas Island red crab lives. These crabs actually live in the forests, not in the sea. They dig burrows in the soil and eat fallen fruits and leaves. But once a year, they swarm in their millions to the coast, to breed and lay their eggs in the sea.

Antarctica

Antarctica is a very unusual continent. It lies around the South Pole, the world's most southerly point, and is the coldest place on Earth, with temperatures dropping as low as −89° Celsius (−128° Fahrenheit). Brrrrrrr! Antarctica has no countries, and no one lives there permanently – although people often go to visit it, or stay for a while to study it. It also has very few animals, as it's so bleak, windy and icy-cold that it's difficult to survive there.

WEDDELL SEA

SOUTHERN OCEAN

Antarctic Peninsula

Ronne Ice Shelf

•
Vinson Massif,
Antarctica's highest point

West Antarctic Ice Sheet

Ross Ice Shelf

AMUNDSEN SEA

Habitats

Not all experts agree on how to describe the habitat of Antarctica. Some say it is a snow and ice habitat, like the top of a high mountain. Some say it's the world's biggest desert, because it's so cold that the water there is almost always frozen into ice and snow, making it a very dry place. Often, the habitat here is simply called "The Antarctic habitat".

Frozen land and snow: The frozen swamplands of the Arctic

Mountains

Seashore and oceans

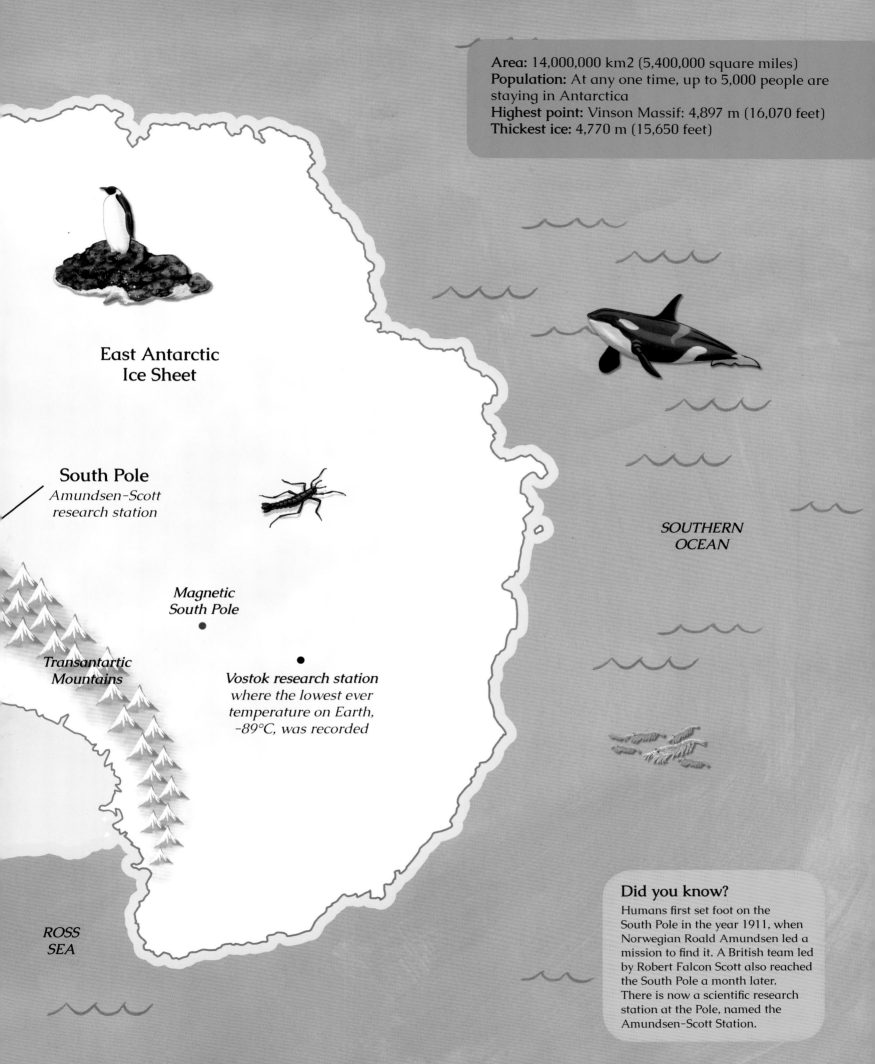

Area: 14,000,000 km2 (5,400,000 square miles)
Population: At any one time, up to 5,000 people are staying in Antarctica
Highest point: Vinson Massif: 4,897 m (16,070 feet)
Thickest ice: 4,770 m (15,650 feet)

**East Antarctic
Ice Sheet**

South Pole
*Amundsen-Scott
research station*

*Magnetic
South Pole*

*Transantartic
Mountains*

*Vostok research station
where the lowest ever
temperature on Earth,
-89°C, was recorded*

*SOUTHERN
OCEAN*

*ROSS
SEA*

Did you know?

Humans first set foot on the
South Pole in the year 1911, when
Norwegian Roald Amundsen led a
mission to find it. A British team led
by Robert Falcon Scott also reached
the South Pole a month later.
There is now a scientific research
station at the Pole, named the
Amundsen-Scott Station.

Antarctica:
Land, ice shelf and ocean

Most of Antarctica's animals live in the sea, or partly in the sea, as it's much easier to find food there – especially shrimp-like creatures called krill which become food for whales and many other animals. Only a few animals come ashore to breed, and even fewer spend their whole lives on the ice-covered land.

Orca

Orcas are found in all the world's oceans, but they're especially common around Antarctica, where they hunt fish and squid in the sea, and seals and penguins around the ice and rocky shores. They're also known as "killer whales", but are actually the world's biggest type of dolphin. They are very clever animals, and live in family groups so that they can help each other to hunt.

Crabeater seal

The crabeater is the most common seal in the world. The seals hunt in the sea, but climb out onto the ice to rest, huddle together, and have their babies. Sometimes, they wander far inland, away from the sea, but no one knows why. Despite their name, crabeater seals mainly eat krill. They have special teeth that let them sieve krill out of the water.

Emperor penguin

Penguins are found in many places, including Australia, New Zealand and Africa. Only Adelie and Emperor penguins actually spend time on Antarctica. Emperor penguins travel as far as 100 kilometres (60 miles) on to the sea ice to lay their eggs. The male and female take turns caring for the egg and chick, giving each other time to trek back to the sea to feed.

Antarctic springtail

Springtails are tiny insects that are found all over the world. They have no wings, but can jump by flicking their tails, and feed on algae and fungi. In Antarctica, springtails are one of the few animals that spend their whole lives on land.

Wingless midge

A type of wingless midge called *Belgica antarctica* is Antarctica's largest true land animal – it grows to six millimetres long, the size of one grain of rice! The midge's larvae, or young, live for two years and can survive being deep-frozen, while the adults only live for a few days during the summer. They feed on algae and moss.

Antarctic krill

Antarctic krill are related to prawns and lobsters, and are around seven centimetres (three inches) long. They swim around in the ocean in massive swarms, feeding on plankton in the water. A bathtub-sized amount of Antarctic seawater is likely to contain up to 2,000 krill.

Glossary

algae Plant-like living things.

alpine To do with mountains, or another name for the montane habitat.

amphibian Animal such as a frog or toad, that can breathe air but usually lays eggs in water.

archipelago A group of islands.

atolls A circular island made of coral that surrounds an area of sea water (lagoon).

bacteria A type of tiny living thing that is not a plant or an animal.

carnivore A living thing that eats meat.

chaparral Another name for the Mediterranean biome.

conifer An evergreen tree that produces fruit in the form of cones.

delta A place where a river slows down and divides into many channels.

domesticate To bring animals or plants under control of humans.

dorsal fin The fin on the back of a fish, whale or dolphin.

endangered Animals or plants that may not exist soon as there are a limited number alive now.

endemic Belonging to and only found in one particular place.

equator Imaginary circle around the Earth, exactly between the two poles.

feral Previously tame, but escaped into the wild.

fertilizer A natural or chemical substance spread on the ground to make plants grow.

guano Droppings, especially those of seabirds or bats.

habitat The particular type of surroundings that an animal lives in.

hibernate To hide away and sleep or rest during the winter.

hydrothermal vent Hole in the seabed where hot water escapes from underground.

inhospitable A place which is not welcoming.

iridescent Sparkling with rainbow-like colours.

isthmus A narrow strip of land joining two larger land masses.

larvae Eggs laid by insects.

mammal Warm-blooded animal that feeds its young on milk.

Mediterranean A bushy, dry biome, named after the land around the Mediterranean Sea.

migrate To move from one place to another.

minerals Chemicals found in the Earth's rocks, such as metals and precious stones.

monotreme Type of mammal that lays eggs.

montane To do with mountains, or a name for the mountain biome.

New World Another name for North, Central and South America.

pampas A type of windy grassland with tall grasses.

peninsula A narrow finger of land sticking out into the sea.

pine An evergreen tree with needle shaped leaves.

plankton Tiny plants and animals that float around in seawater.

plateau A high, flat area of land.

plumes A large feather.

prairie A type of grassland.

prehensile Type of tail that can be used to wrap around and hold onto branches or other objects.

prehistoric From the time before history began to be written down.

reef Area of coral, rock or sand that lies just under the surface of the sea.

reptile Type of cold-blooded, air-breathing animal, such as a snake, lizard or crocodile.

rodent Type of small mammal with large gnawing front teeth, such as a mouse, rat or squirrel.

roost To settle down and rest or sleep in a tree, on a cave wall or somewhere high up.

saliva Liquid produced in your mouth to keep it wet and get it ready for food.

savanna A type of dry grassland dotted with trees.

species A particular type of living thing.

steppe A type of temperate grassland.

subspecies Different types of an animal within the same species.

taiga Cold biome made up of conifer forests.

temperate Medium-warm, not extremely cold or hot.

tropical To do with the tropics, the warm area of the Earth around the equator.

tundra Cold habitat featuring boggy, frozen ground and low-growing plants.

venom A poisonous liquid produced by some snakes and insects when they bite or sting.

wilderness Wild, natural landscape that has not been altered by humans.

Index

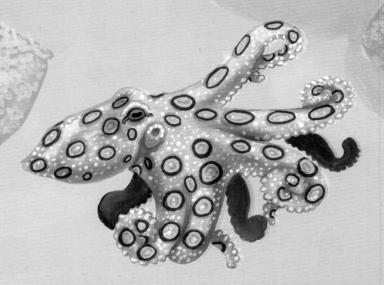